How to Play Pool

Guide

Contents

Your Cue stick	1
Holding a Cue stick	1
Rear Hand Grip Position	1
Front Hand Bridge	1
Open Bridge	2
Closed Bridge	3
A stable Bridge	3
Bridge Positioning	4
Shooting from a Rail.	5
Stroke	6
Grip of the Rear hand	6
Arm Swing	7
Stance	7
Practice Strokes	7
Contact with the Cue ball	9
Practice your stroke	9
Aiming	10
Chalking the Stick	10
The Cue Ball	11
Hitting the center of the Cue ball	11
English	11
Bottom (reverse) English	12
Top (forward) English.	13
Side (left right) English	13
Practicing English	14
Beginners Conclusion.	14
Practice lessons #1	14
Stroke Accuracy	15
Practicing English	16

For Beginners and Intermediate Players

Playing the Game	17
The Game of 8-Ball	17
The Game of 9-Ball	17
Natural Rolls	18
Approaching 90 Degrees	20
Practice lessons #2	23
Altering the Natural Roll	22
Practice lessons #3	23
Cue Ball Extremes	24
Shooting Strategies	26
Rails	32

Practice lessons #4 34
Altering the mirror image angle 37
Tips on Improving your game. 38
    The Power Break 38
    After the Break 39
Planning for the simple run 41
Using the Bridge Stick 47

For Advanced Shooters

The 8-Ball Break 47
Hard Shots vs. Easy shots 49
Breakouts 49
Safeties. 49
    Hiding behind two balls that are tied up . . 50
    Hiding behind two balls out on an open table. . . 51
    Hiding the cue behind another ball . . . 52
Masse' Shots 53
    Hitting a masse' shot 53
    General purpose Masse' Shot 54
    Long Range Masse' Shot 54
    Aiming A Masse' Shot 55
Jump Shots 55
Throwing a ball 56
Making that Pesky Ball-off-the-Rail Shot 57
Double Rail Shots 58
Caroms 58
    Transference 60
Action and Reaction 62

For All Players

Cue Stick Maintenance 64
    Scuffing the tip 64
    The Shape of the Tip 64
    Removing dings in the shaft 64
Practice games 64

Your Cue Stick:

The most important tool used to play pool is the cue stick. Without it we'd be poking the cueball with our fingers. Which, by the way, doesn't work and is hard on the fingertips.

First we need to select the weight of our cue stick. Cue sticks come in a variety of weights from 16 - 23 ounces. The average is between 19 – 21 ounces. On one end of the scale the lighter sticks can apply greater "English", (we will learn this later in this book, in general "English" is spin on the cueball). Where heavier sticks have greater breaking power, and are easier to control. I just happen to prefer a 20.5-ounce stick.

When starting out playing pool, a beginner would be better off with a heavier stick. But it is still your decision on what feels comfortable to you. A heavier stick will keep your arm swinging straighter and not require as much muscle to move a ball around the table.

"But why would 2 or 3 ounces make such a difference? The answer to this is the weight of the cue ball. Most cue balls only weigh between 5.5 to 6 ounces, so that extra 2-3 ounces hitting the cue ball can make a significant difference.

When learning how to stroke it is better using a heavier cue stick so you do not have to use much force to move a ball, the cue sticks' weight will do that for you. The lighter the hit the more control you have over it.

Holding a Cue Stick:

Rear Hand Grip Position:
Your position on the cue stick will vary depending on your height. Taller people will generally hold their cue stick more toward the rear of the "Grip" area (for most sticks the "Grip" area is defined as the area near the rear of the stick with some kind of wrap around it). Shorter people will generally hold it closer to the front of this area. The average person 5'7" to 6' should hold their stick in the middle of this area or just to the rear of middle.

Front Hand Bridge:
The "Bridge" is formed by your front hand, and is to rest the cue stick on during the stroke. There are two trains of thought on this. The "Open Bridge" where the thumb and first finger form a small "V" shape to rest the front of the stick in, and the "Closed

Bridge" method where the first finger coils around the cue stick and the tip of the finger rests on your thumb. We will discuss both and the advantages and disadvantages to each.

a. The Open Bridge:
While this method offers better sighting down the cue stick, most professionals use the "Closed Bridge" method, this is only because they have been playing long enough that they do not need much stick to sight in their shots. The Open Bridge is a good method for beginners to use to get better, faster. While the "Closed Bridge" hides bad habits the "Open Bridge" exposes them quickly.

Below are pictures of the use of the Open Bridge Method.

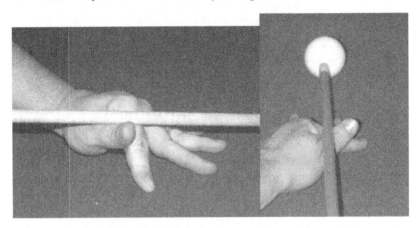

This method allows the beginner to medium skilled player to see the line of the shot better. It also allows the shooter to observe the movement of his stick before, during and after his shot. To achieve this bridge is very simple. Lay your hand flat on the table, fingers spread widely but not uncomfortably. Lift your thumb until your first knuckle just lifts up off the table, about 1/2 inch. Do not lift your palm from the table. Now move your thumb forward until it meets your first finger just below the knuckle, forming a small "V" shape. The cue stick will rest in the "V" shape. This is a very stable platform for your stick.

This method allows a beginner to observe the movement of the stick to and from the ball as your stroking the stick back and forth. If side-to-side wiggle is observed at the tip of the stick, this means your arm is not swinging like a pendulum. What wiggle observed, is being done by the back hand during your swing. The wiggle at the tip is 1/5 of what your back arm is doing. If you notice an arcing motion as you stroke this is caused by a misalignment of your arm to the stick.

We will discuss more of this throughout the next chapters.

b. The Closed Bridge:

While this is a preferred method, as it offers more control over the end of the cue stick, it can be a hindrance to beginners learning how to aim. In a closed bridge your own finger blocks some of the view of the stick. The closed bridge method keeps the pool stick from raising during the shot, which can help shooters. However it is only masking the fact that the shooters swing is not the best it can be and he is probably holding the rear of the cue stick too tightly. When reviewing the open bridge photos above you can easily see right down the shaft of the stick to the cue ball. But as shown in the photo below, you have a somewhat obstructed view down the shaft to the cue ball. This small obstruction can cause the shooter to judge incorrectly exactly where he is aiming.

Below is a picture the proper Closed Bridge.

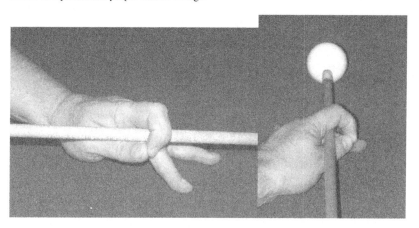

A Closed Bridge is formed by laying your hand flat on the table, fingers spread widely but not uncomfortably. Curl your first finger and rest the fingertip on the side of the thumb, doing this lifts the knuckles up off the table about 1/2 inch. Do not lift your palm from the table. Now move your thumb up until a cue stick can pass through resting on your thumb side. This wrapping of your finger around the stick must not interfere with the movement of the stick during your stroke, so it must remain loose around the stick.

A Stable Bridge:

You will notice that on both the open and closed bridges the fingers are spread widely. This spreading of the fingers allows for a very stable bridge. A stable bridge and a good stroke is at the very heart of learning to play pool and getting better quickly.

During game play you will need to raise and lower your bridge to shoot the shot and English needed. To do this, simply turn your wrist. Do not lift your fingertips from the table. You will notice by turning your wrist, the rest for the cue stick raises up and down, and your fingertips slide in and out. When raising up keeping the fingers spread as you turn your wrist will cause your fingers to become legs on which your Bridge stands. When a lower bridge is used most of the bridge rests on the palm of your hand.

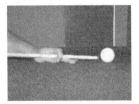 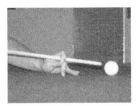

The left picture shows the closed bridge in the lower state, while the right picture show the bridge in the raised state.

Keeping your fingertips touching the table, spread as far apart as is comfortable, is essential to a good shot. The next thing to discuss is "Where do I put my hand when I go to shoot".

Bridge Positioning:
The best and most accurate shooting occurs when a comfortable, stable bridge can be made ~9" away from the cueball. A further explanation of this is that the "V" shape in which the cue stick rests is about 9 inches from the cueball. Your fingertips may be much closer than that.

The picture below shows the proper distances:

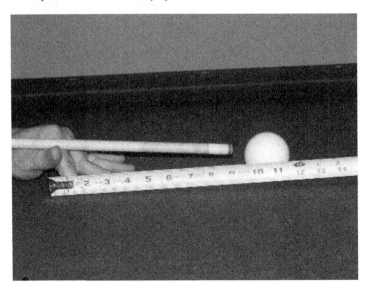

This 9" distance is based on the amount of swing your arm can provide (without hyper-extension), the ratio of the length of your stick in front of the bridge and the length of the stick behind the bridge, and the weight balance of the stick. When the cue is resting with your back arm in the straight up and down position, the tip of the cue should be 1/2" – 3/4" away from the cue ball.

Shooting from a Rail:
It would be nice to always have that room to make a good bridge, but a lot of the time you will need to shoot from the rail. This is the only time you should deviate from the 9" distance. Shown below are some of the proper methods of shooting off the rail.

In the first picture, the palm is rested on the rail; the fingers are still spread widely and are used to adjust the bridge up or down. The 9" distance is still in use here, only the palm is up onto the rail.

In this picture we can see the fingers now curl under the rail gripping it lightly to hold a steady bridge, rotate the wrist to adjust up or down. The 9" distance should still be adhered to.

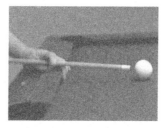

In the next picture, we see the cue ball is too close to the rail to shoot anything other than top English. The palm of the hand is actually off the table, the fingers are spread apart laying on the table, the first finger in pointing down on the edge of the table. This finger acts as a stop holding the hand firmly in place while the thumb and this finger acts as our open bridge.

Twisting of the wrist raises and lowers the bridge; the key to shooting these shots accurately is to raise the bridge enough that the tip of the cue just clears the felt. The photo below shows the perfect angle to hit a ball very close if not actually touching the rail; any lower of an angle and you will skip off the top of the ball in a miscue. This is the only time when we are unable to get the 9" distance recommended, as the rails on most tables are about 6 – 8" wide.

Stroke:
The stroke of the cue stick is the second most important factor in the game of pool. Even if your aim is perfect, your stroke can alter it enough to miss your shot. A good stroke is achieved by a relaxed hand and forearm.

  a. Grip of the Rear hand:

The grip on the cue stick should be in the middle of the grip area (again this changes with height of the shooter). It should be gripped loosely, but able to hold the stick as the arm swings.

The thumb and first finger do most of the holding of the stick, while the middle finger and next finger provide support for the stick. The pinky finger should not do much, it's like drinking tea, extend the pinky to look high class!!

Below is a picture of the correct grip:

b. Arm Swing

Once we have the grip down, now we need to learn how to swing our arms. The stroke is greatly affected by the way your arm swings. The elbow should be above your back slightly, with the forearm hanging down straight, swinging in a pendulum fashion.

During the stroke and after the shot, the elbow should remain frozen in place. The angle of your arm and the stick should be aligned with each other, so that the swing of the arm does not alter the side-to-side position of the cue tip.

c. Stance

Remember that 9 inch distance, it now comes into play. Your rear hand grips exact position will depend on your arm hanging straight down with your other arm out to that 9 inch position. By doing this, it should have turned you somewhat sideways, now bend over until your chin is ¼" from resting on the stick. If your front hand is not in the 9 inch position, move your rear hand grip backward or forward slightly, until this stance and distance is achieved.

Notice that the feet are spread for a comfortable stance, and that the body is about 45 degrees to the stick. This allows a comfortable stance, maximum sighting down the cue, and proper swing of the cue during the stroke.

The swinging of the rear arm moves the cue stick forward and backward in your bridge. The 9 inch distance should be just enough that as your arm swings back to around 45 degrees, the tip of the stick will be about and 1 or 2 inches from your bridge. During the stroke while sighting down the stick, the stick should be moving smoothly back and forth with NO side-to-side wiggle.

d. Practice strokes

Now swinging your arm from ~45 degrees down to 90 degrees will move the cue stick back and forth. Examine at your swing and look at the travel of the stick. It should be straight and smooth.

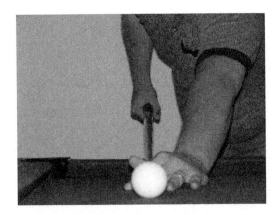

The picture above shows the alignment of the rear arm to the stick; notice that the arm is aligned with the stick.

Proper alignment between the stick and your arm will keep the cue tip from swinging in an arcing motion. See the illustrations below; illustration #2 is the perfect stroke.

Illustration #1   Illustration #2   Illustration #3

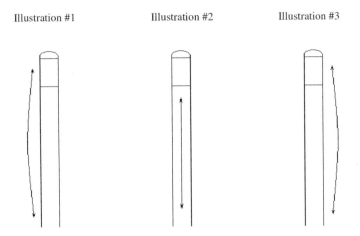

In illustration #1 and #3 we see what it looks like if our arm is not aligned properly, our arm is not swinging in a straight pendulum fashion. This can be caused by your stance being to sideways, standing almost parallel to your stick. Or your stance being not angled enough and standing almost 90 degrees to your stick.

Another cause can be your arm is tucked in too tightly to your body or sticking out too far. Illustration #1 is most likely to be your arm stuck out too far. Illustration #3's most likely cause is your arm tucked in too tightly to your body.

Contact with the Cue ball:

When you feel comfortable in your practice strokes, the stroke is then continued forward until your arm is ~20 - 30 degrees forward. This forward movement, past your arm being straight down, is the contact portion of the stroke. It is during a level portion of your stroke when we contact the cue ball. This provides the maximum control over the hit. During the application of English this is critical.

The degree measurements given here are not absolute. They are merely guidelines to use. If the stroke stays within these guidelines, the stroke will be level and clean. If you go too far backward or forward during your stroke, the front tip of the cue stick will dip downwards sharply. This is easily seen with the open bridge, and is recommended that this be observed while practicing your stroke.

Practice your stroke:

Take about the next half hour practicing your swing. You should practice in front of a mirror so you can observe your swing. The arm swings like a pendulum the elbow does not move up or down. The cue stick is level and straight, and the cue tip travel is straight in and out.

Now that we have learned to stroke we need to learn how to aim our stroke.

Aiming:
Aiming is done by sighting down the cue stick through the cue ball, to the location needed. Notice I did not say aiming at the "point of contact" because this is a mistake made by most beginners, to intermediate players.

There is a difference between where you aim, and the point of contact. The point of contact is where the cue ball contacts the object ball to make it go the direction you want it to go. While the location of your aiming, is exactly ½ the cue balls diameter from that point!

See the drawing below to illustrate this example.

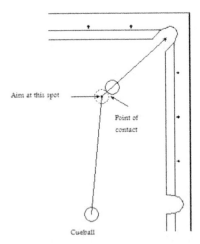

For proper aiming you must imagine a cueball sitting next to the object ball touching the object ball in a straight line with where you want the object ball to go. Now aim for the center of that imaginary ball. This is an accurate aiming technique for every shot on the table, except for kick shots. A kick shot is where the cue ball is aimed for the rail first, to then bounce off the rail to hit that "imaginary" cue ball.

Chalking the Stick:
Now that we've learned to aim your going to want to start hitting balls around, so we better cover this now.

The tip of the cue stick is made from leather, and will need the application of chalk to achieve accurate hits on the cue ball. I recommend chalking between each shot. This gives you time to think about your shot, and keeps the tip in good condition. See Cue Stick Maintenance.

The Cue Ball

The cue ball is very predictable in its travels, until you start using English. When the cue ball it contacted by the cue stick, the ball will slide forward until the friction of the felt causes the ball to start rolling. This friction is a very important part of the game. (You will hear advanced players saying, "This is a fast table" this simply means that the felt has less friction than what they are used to) The amount of friction a tables' felt has, directly affects the amount of English the cue ball will "take".

Hitting the Center of the Cue ball:

When a cue ball is hit normal (center of the ball), it slides a small distance then starts to roll. Depending on this amount of spin the ball picks up from the table, will determine how far beyond the point of contact the cue ball will roll. For instance if you shoot at an object ball that is 3 feet away, unless you slam the cueball, it will start rolling forward by the time it reaches the object ball. Depending on the power applied to the cueball, the cueball will continue to roll forward for some distance after contact. If you shoot straight at a ball only 6 inches away depending, on the power applied, it will likely be in the slide portion of the shot and will cause the cue ball to stop dead once it contacts the object ball.

English:

Simply put "English" is not shooting the cue ball directly through the center of the ball. Anywhere other than directly in the center of the ball (as you see it looking down your stick) is going to apply "English", to some extent. It may surprise you to know that you can hit the cueball off to the side of the ball by as much as ½", and still have it travel forward in the direction you aimed! However, what you have done is applied a sideways spin to the cue ball. This spin does have its benefits and drawbacks to it. The first drawback is if not properly hit, you will miscue by having the tip of your stick bounce off the cue ball, and the cue ball go rolling in some weird direction. English is one of the tools available to the more experienced shooters.

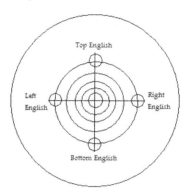

Any of the rings, other than the center circle, is English.

Bottom (reverse) English:

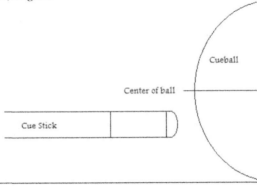

Bottom English is the most Basic English, and the one most abused by the majority of the intermediate shooters. Bottom English is exactly what it sounds like. It is hitting the cueball below the center as in the drawing above.

This English applied to the cueball causes the ball to spin backward. This English applied with sufficient power, will cause the cueball to spin the entire distance it travels forward, until it hits the object ball. If spin still remains on the cue ball it will then start to back-up away from the point of contact.

If played properly and only enough force is applied to the cueball to spin the ball backward until point of contact, the cue ball will stop dead once contact is made with the object ball. Bottom English will only last until the friction of traveling across the table felt, is more than the power applied.

Once the friction has stopped the reverse spin, the cue ball will slide for a small amount of time, and then begin to spin forward as it rolls. This friction can be used to your advantage, skilled players are able to use this friction to achieve shot positioning that would normally be impossible to achieve.

For instance, a ball must be shot into the side pocket but to get the next shot it can not roll more than 3 inches forward from the point of contact. To hit it slowly would not give the object ball enough power to reach the pocket. But to hit it hard enough for the object ball to make it into the side pocket would cause the cue ball to roll forward too far. Putting too much bottom English on it would cause the ball to stop dead or back up from point of contact and this would not give us our next shot either.

So what to do? Using the friction of the table a skilled player can hit it with enough power to make the shot but have the reverse English just wear off a few inches before the point of contact. Thus allowing the ball to just start rolling forward before it hits the object ball. This slight rolling forward motion allows the cue ball to continue to roll forward only a small amount thus giving us our next shot.

Top (forward) English:

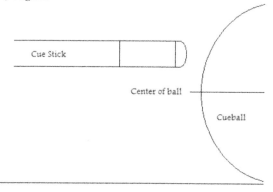

Forward English is hitting the ball above the center of the ball. This causes the ball to actually spin faster forward than it normally would rolling forward. This English applied with sufficient power, will cause the cue ball to spin, the entire distance it travels forward until it hits the object ball. If spin still remains on the cue ball it will then continue to roll forward from the point of contact.

Top English will only last until the friction of traveling across the table felt is more than the power applied. Once the friction has stopped the excess forward spin, the cue ball will begin to spin forward normally as it rolls.

Side (left, right) English:

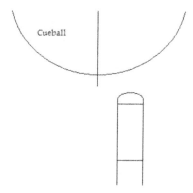

Side English is more often used by the more advanced shooters. By the use of side English, or a mix of side and top or bottom, will make the cue ball spin on a tilted axis. This tilted axis can be used to make the cue ball go in a more radically different direction then it was meant to. We will look at the use of English in playing shots later in this book.

Practicing English:
To learn the use of English take a striped ball, and use it as your cue ball, lining up the stripe around the ball, parallel with the table. Hit the ball in the center of the ball and watch the stripe. You will notice the ball sliding forward for a split second, before the ball starts rolling forward. Now try lining up the ball again, use bottom English and notice the stripe spinning backwards for some distance, before appearing to stop, and then start spinning forward. Now try lining up the ball again, this time using top English. This is extremely hard to see the subtle difference between the ball just rolling forward, and spinning forward as it travels.

Beginners Conclusion:
We have now studied how to hold the stick, and stroke the cue ball. This is where you will use the practice lessons below and go practice for a couple of weeks.
Good luck to you, and have fun.

Practice Lessons #1

Stroke Accuracy:
Following diagram shows how we will practice our stroke accuracy. Place two balls on the rail on opposite sides of the center diamond, the cue ball should be able to fit between them with about 1/8th of inch on either side. Place the cue ball lined up with the center diamonds. Your going to practice hitting the cue ball between the two other balls without touching them and have the cue ball come right back to your stick. Practice this until you are able to do this 4 out of every 5 times

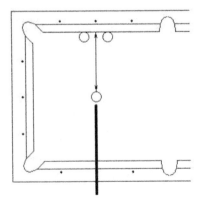

Practicing English:

Bottom (reverse) English:
In the diagram below we are going to practice shooting with bottom English. We are going to learn control of our English speed.

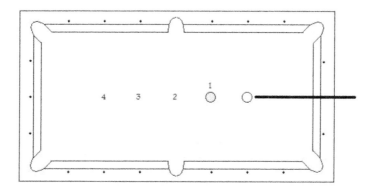

With the cue ball lined up to the center diamonds. We put a ball one diamond away (#1 position). We then stroke the cue ball with bottom English; the object of this lesson is to stop the cue ball dead as soon as it hits the object ball.

Once we have mastered our shot at position #1 move the object ball to position #2, then to #3 and #4. You must be able to stop the ball within ½ inch of the point of contact at each of these locations.

This teaches us accuracy, speed, power, and bottom English, keep practicing until at positions 1 and 2 you can do this consistently (4 out of 5 times) and at positions 3 and 4 you are able to stop the ball 1 out of every 2 times.

Top (Forward) English:

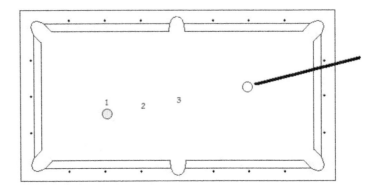

In this diagram we are going to practice forward English. With the cue ball lined up with the center diamonds we use forward English to roll the cue ball to the rail.

Note: we are shooting at and angle to keep the object ball from bouncing back into our cue ball.

The object is to hit the object ball as straight as possible and have the cue ball follow it and hit the rail on the end of the table and bounce back no further than the first diamond. You start with the object ball at position 1 once you have mastered this one (4 out of 6 times), move the object ball to position 2 then 3. This teaches us Accuracy, speed, power, and top English. You will have mastered it when you can make cue ball within the area from position 3, 1 out of every 3 times.

You will need to practice these fundamentals by switching from one practice lesson to the other until you have mastered each. These are the learning blocks that will build your game quickly and make you an above average player. So please take your time and learn each before moving to the next section.

For beginners and intermediate players

The following section advances us to the intermediate player. I hope you had fun practicing and learning to stroke and using English. In the next section we will talk about what happens when we hit the cue ball in to the object ball and how it effects how we play the game.

Playing the Game:
There are many games to play on the pool table. These are the most popular.

The Game of 8-Ball:
The game of 8-Ball is played with all 15 balls in a triangular rack of balls. The 8-ball must be located in the center of the triangle. The first person shoots the cue ball in to the rack; this is called the "Break". This causes the balls to scatter. Once the balls are scattered, if a ball went into a pocket, the person who broke is allowed to shoot again.

Some rules allow the shooter to choose the ball set (Solids or Stripes) that he wants at this point. While some rules dictate he take the set of the ball(s) he made during the break. If a ball is not made on the break, the other shooter is allowed his turn, and is given the choice of shooting any ball set he wants.

The shooters continue their turn until a shot is not made. Then the other player shoots until he misses. This rotation is continued until one player has made all his set (1-7 if solid, 9-15 if stripes) then he is allowed to shoot the 8-ball. The sinking of the 8 ball concludes the game.

The Game of 9-Ball:
In the game of 9-ball the balls are racked 1-9 in a diamond shape, with the 1 ball in front and 9 ball in the center. The breaker must hit the one ball first to break. After the break, the balls must be shot in their numerical order. The game is won when the 9-ball is sunk.

The 9 ball can be made out of order to win the game, but only if the next numerical ball was hit first, to be a valid shot. For example, someone can shoot the one ball into the nine ball, causing the nine ball to be pocketed. This would conclude the game.

In both these games, the way to win is to make all your balls before the opponent makes their balls. So a primary strategy of the game is to keep them from making their balls first. This can be done by a shooting strategy.

A Professional player can easily be beaten in a game of pool, if he never gets a shot. So this is where we start to discuss shooting and the reactions of the cue ball after a shot. Understanding the reaction of the cue ball is essential to developing a playing strategy to get to the next shot. The first reaction to understand is the natural roll of the cue ball.

In the next section we cover the natural roll of the cue ball.

Natural Rolls:

When shooting a ball into another ball the cue ball will tend to continue rolling forward for some distance, unless an English is used. This is called a "Natural Roll", because we did nothing to alter the natural course of the cue ball. When hitting a ball at an angle, the angle the cue ball will deflect off the object ball is very predictable.

Shown below are some natural angles:

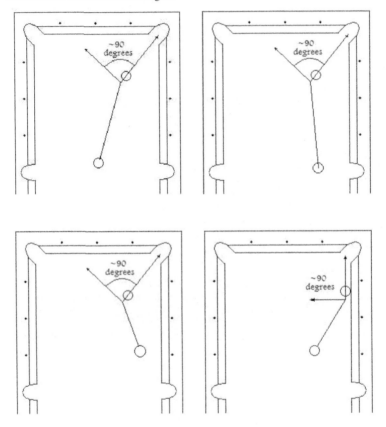

As you can see most of the time the cue ball will come off at a 90 degree angle to the angle of the object balls direction once hit. This however is not true for a small portion of the time.

When a shot is made from within the striped area, as in the diagram below, the cue ball's natural roll will continue to roll forward at an angle ~3 times the angular difference between the cue balls intended path and the object balls path.

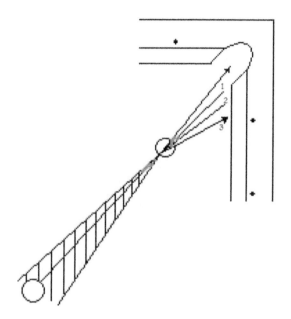

The arrowed line pointing into the pocket represents the path of the object ball into the pocket. The second line represents the path of the cue ball, actually the intended path if the object ball was not there.

This small angle between those lines (the angle area marked with the #1) is multiplied by 3, represented by angle areas #1, #2 and #3. The area between lines 2 and line #3 is where you have the natural roll. During a normal firm hit the arrowed #3 line is the natural path of the cue ball after the hit.

Due to this multiplying effect, you can see that a small distance outside the shaded area will multiply up to the 90 degrees rather quickly. As illustrated in the drawing on the next page. The 90 degrees is the maximum angle of deflection, until an English is used.

Hitting the ball softer or harder will change this angle also. A soft hit will closely follow line #2 a harder shot will increase this to the arrowed line #3. Once at 90 degrees hard or soft will not matter it will travel at the 90 degree line.

Approaching 90 degrees:
   In this drawing we see that the angle multiplied out quickly to almost 90 degrees

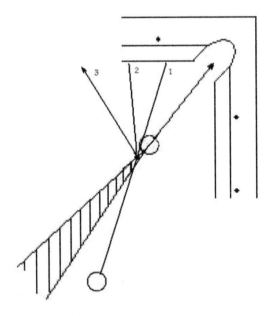

   We are going to practice some natural rolls by following the lessons on the next page. Setup your shots and practice until you can fairly accurately predict where the cue ball is going to go each time you shoot.
   This is a very critical step in your learning process. Take as much time as you need to learn this.

   Again the natural roll is for a medium shot strength with NO english on the cue ball. Shooting harder will always follow the third angle but still max'ed out at 90 degrees. In the diagram above it is almost at the 90 degrees so a hard or soft shot will still basically follow the #3 arrowed line.

Practice Lessons #2:

In this practice lesson we use the cue ball and two other balls. Your going to setup a small shot just like the diagram below. The object of the lesson is to make the object ball and have the cue ball roll into the second ball.

Diagram #1 Try different positions for the cue ball.

Diagram #2 Don't put the cue ball too close to the object ball, or it wont roll forward.

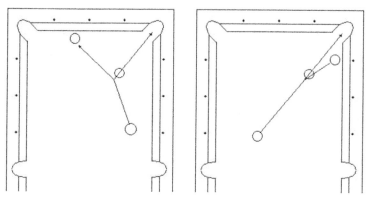

Diagram #3 Try angles from about 20 to 40 degrees, make sure the object ball is on the rail.

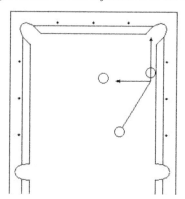

Altering a Natural Roll:

Now you may have practiced the shots above and missed the second ball completely, but did what you thought was the same shot and hit the second ball on the next try. Well, this is because we can bend or alter these naturals angles by the use of top and bottom English.

This is how the pros make in look so easy, they can alter the natural rolls of the cue ball to avoid trapping themselves. They can use the altered course to break out trapped balls as well as preventing a scratch.

The illustrations below show the same shot represented in the examples above, but show the altered ball paths.

See below:

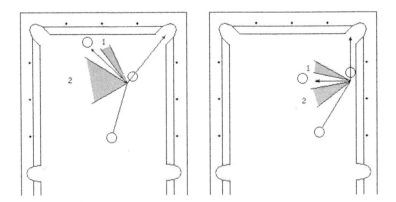

The shaded areas are the possible areas the ball could have traveled. Area #1 is the use of top English or a very soft shot (Soft shots tend to mimic forward english because they are rolling forward immediately after being hit). The top (forward) English tends to push the ball more forward of the natural roll. While bottom (reverse) English tends to try and reverse the ball so it comes out in area #2 behind the natural roll. Shooting very hard and moving into the fourth angle may have cause your ball to miss also in the #2 area.

This bending or altering of the natural angles can be very useful for avoiding a scratch (pocketing the cue ball) or breaking out a trapped ball. But you must understand the natural rolls first, before you can understand how to alter them to what you need.

This next set of practice lessons allow us to experiment with English and our recently learned knowledge of the natural roll.

Practice Lessons #3:

Try the practice lessons below to learn about altering the natural angles. In the lessons below you are going to try NOT to hit the second ball but instead you want to consistently miss the second ball while still making your shot. Remember 1's are top English, 2's are bottom English.

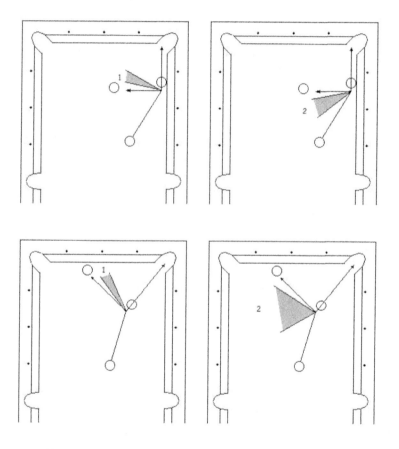

This next section is more for fun than for learning, but you will get an idea of some things that can be done.

Cue ball Extremes:

When extreme English is applied properly the cue ball can do some pretty amazing things. Shown below are some diagrams of simple extreme English cue ball movements, all the way to some really tricky and amazing shots.

This example shows how extreme Top (forward) English can actually curve the cue ball around another ball to make a second ball. The secret to this shot is the amount of power applied to the cue ball. When the hits the first object ball it literally bounces off the rail toward the center of the table until the forward English wants to move it forward again. This bounce and forward English struggling against each other causes the curving effect.

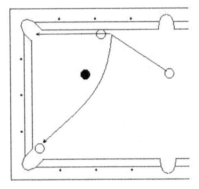

In this example the first ball is hit into the pocket this slows the cue ball down and changes its angle just enough to bounce of the rail and spin around the blocking ball to make the second ball.

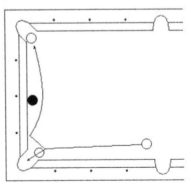

This example shows how extreme bottom (reverse) English causes a ball to curve, the trick to this shot is also the amount of power applied to the cue ball. Since the ball was hit very firmly the cue ball wants to keep moving forward but the spin of the bottom (reverse) English causes it to curve around the blocking ball to make the second ball

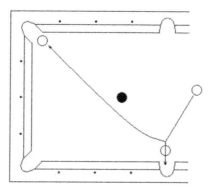

In this example, extreme bottom (reverse) English is used and the cue ball is drawn almost straight backwards taking a small bounce of the rail just before making the second ball.

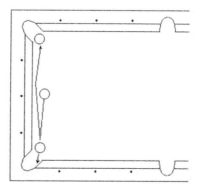

Shooting Strategies:

Ever wonder why the pros make it look so easy? Almost all their shots are easy angles if not straight in shots. It comes down to one basic concept, "Shot Choice". A top player will plan out his entire game before he steps up to the table. I am not asking this of you now. But as you increase your skill level you will look more and more shots ahead in the game.

We are going to take a look at some basic scenarios you will come across in a game, and the best-shot choices for these scenarios. These shot choices will include defense, best-shot layout, and ease of making the shots.

In this diagram we see a shot that comes up a lot in the game, you have two balls to make ball 1 and ball 2. Which one do you take first?

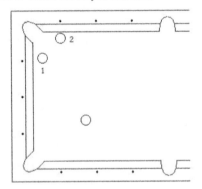

Lets examine the layout of the table first, shown in the illustration below is the table broken up into sections, the object balls are both in section 1 of the table.

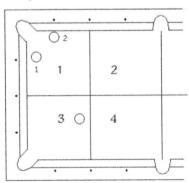

While the cue ball is in section 3, this makes the shot choice obvious, the correct shot choice is ball #1. If the cue ball was in section 2 then the correct choice is ball #2. So what about section 4? Well this gets a little trickier. See the example below

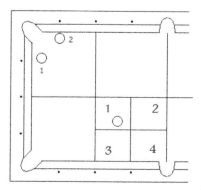

Now section 4 is broken into four smaller sections, and the cue ball is moved to section 1, the correct shot is still ball #1 for section 1,3 and 4. But, when it is in section 2 the correct shot is ball #2.

Why can ball #1 be right for sections 1,3 and 4 but not 2? Isn't it about a 50/50 shot choice? Absolutely not, Ball #1 is slightly off the rail more than Ball #2, this makes it a slightly easier shot to make. Now we show why this shot choice is the correct one. In the diagram below we are shooting the ball in and seeing where the cue ball goes.

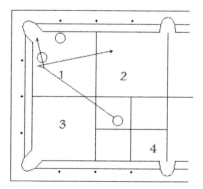

After our shot we see why this was the proper choice, the natural roll puts us into section 2 giving us a nice easy shot.

In this scenario, again it is a shot we will see over and over again in a game. We have three balls to shoot two on one side a one on the other side. So which is the proper shot choice, 1,2 or 3?

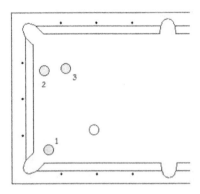

This is a shot that a lot of the intermediate players will still make a mistake on. Most players make the mistake of shooting #1 because it is the easiest. Well let's see what that will get us.

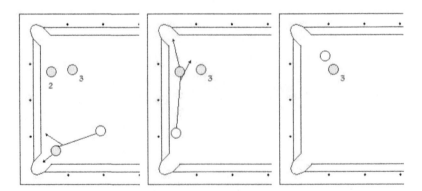

Now we see the trap that was set for us. Of course, using English can change this scenario greatly, however we are looking at the easiest way to do this, not trying to use English to get us out of a situation we should have never gotten into in the first place! In the above scenario we now have no shot for the #3 ball or a much harder shot than needed.

The solution to the above scenario is shooting ball #3 to start with. Follow in illustrations below.

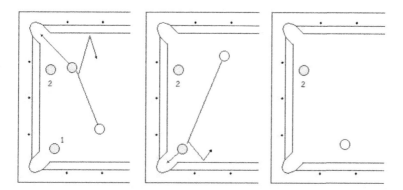

Now we see why this is the best shot choice, there are no hidden traps the natural rolls take us to nice easy shots for the next ball. So lets recap this lesson, if you have a three ball scenario in a game it will be almost always best to pick a ball on the side with two balls.

This is another three ball scenario that occurs a lot, you have only two balls left and the third ball is the 8ball. Obviously ball #1 is the easiest ball to make, but let's examine this.

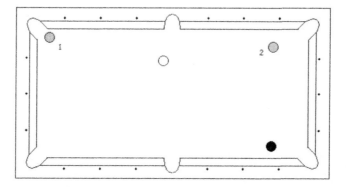

Again this is the same as the three ball example above. The best-shot choice is the harder shot for the #2 ball. But Why? I know I can make that easy #1 ball! Well that's exactly why we don't shoot it!

Instead we shoot at the #2 ball lightly, just hard enough to make it, if it does not go this is where strategy come into play lets examine in the following illustration.

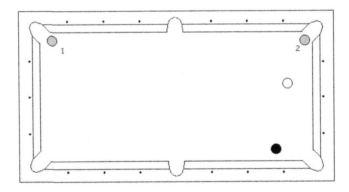

We missed our shot on the #2 ball, but because we shot it lightly the opponent has no shot on the 8-ball. This is why we chose the #2 ball, if we had made it, can we still make that #1 ball? Well of course we can, and once it bounces of the rail it leaves us pretty good for the 8-ball.

One very important strategy to remember, it is sometimes better <u>not</u> to make the ball! Lets examine the scenario below, if we shoot our ball in we will then be forced to shoot at our next ball that has no pocket to go into. If we can even hit it!

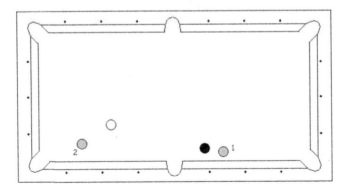

So what do we do? We miss our ball on purpose trying to get it closer to the pocket as in the illustration below:

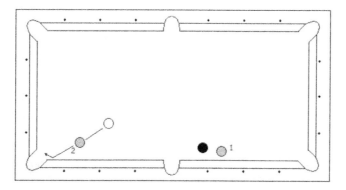

Doing this forces your opponent to shoot the 8-ball. Once he knocks the 8-ball out of your way you have a nice easy ball to make because you left your ball near the pocket. You shoot the easy one and use your roll too setup for the harder one. Examine the illustrations below.

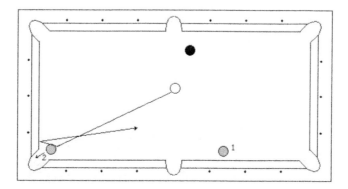

Shoot to roll up the table to get a little closer to your next shot.

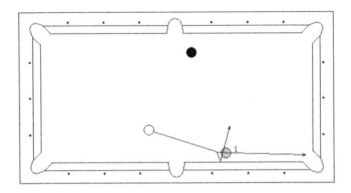

Now you have a nice easy shot on the 8 ball in the side. Now of course you had to make a somewhat hard shot on the #1 ball, but isn't that better than the impossible shot you had if you had made the #2 ball in the first place?

Rails:

I'm not going to get into the multiple rails mathematics. I'm going to keep it simple, only single rail banks. For a single rail bank shot, think of the rail as a mirror. If you have someone who can help you take a handheld mirror and hold it up like the picture below:

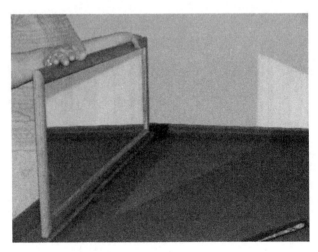

32

When you look into the mirror you can see the ball your aiming at as if it was straight in front of you. This is what a bank off the rail is like. Once you hit the rail, the cue ball comes back off the rail in a mirror image of the angle the cue ball hit the rail with.

See the illustration below:

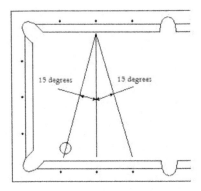

You must hit the ball normal and not hard for it to follow this exact mirror image. Speed and English will alter this angle drastically. Practice this mirror angle using the dots as in the practice lessons below

Practice Lesson #4:

Practice banking from diamond to pocket

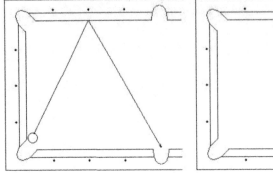

Well all this is good, but I can't carry a mirror around with me while I play pool, and most of the time it does not line up with any dots on the table, now what do I do? Ok so let's use something we are carrying around with us to measure out the shots, Our Stick! Look at illustration #1 this certainly doesn't line up straight, illustration #2 shows it doesn't line up with the dots.

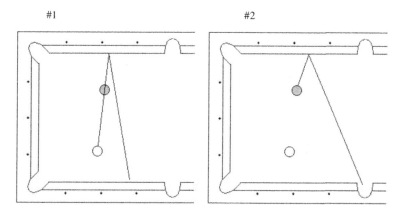

So how can I use my stick to figure out this angle? You figure it out by making a triangle with your stick through the object ball to the rail see the illustration below:

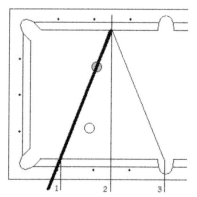

By laying your stick out you can make a triangle to show you where your point of contact is on the object ball. Notice line #2, this line is from one side of the table to the other the distance between your stick and this line is exactly ½ the distance from your stick to the pocket. This shows that this is the correct angle and shows us where we need to hit the object ball to make this bank shot.

Ok, what about a long bank where the cue ball has to be the one going off the rail, what do I do then? Well we still use our stick to measure it, but a little differently.

Put the tip of your stick where you want to hit the object ball to make it in the pocket, measure the distance from the tip of your stick to the rail. Put your finger on your stick to keep this measurement. See Illustration below:

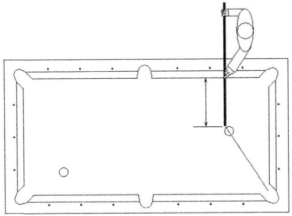

Now slide your stick back until the tip is even with the rail.

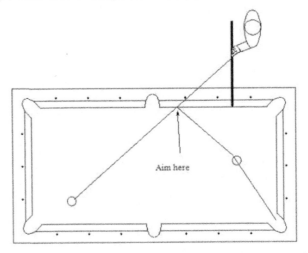

You must keep the stick aligned 90 degrees to the table when doing this. Now look from your finger on the stick to the cue ball, the point at which it crosses the rail is where you aim.

Altering the mirror image angle:
Hitting the ball hard will cause the angle to change; this is due to the compression of the rail when the cue ball hits it. When a speeding cue ball hits the rail, the rail compresses slightly. The rail then recoils, pushing the ball off at a slightly straighter angle than when it hit the rail. See below:

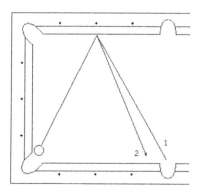

In this example you can see that because we hit it harder instead of following angle 1 it actually followed angle 2. This can be useful when you cannot hit the location you need instead you can aim further away and hit it harder.

For example in the illustration below our natural bank if blocked by your opponents ball, so we aim slightly beyond it and hit it harder, straightening out the angle and making our ball.

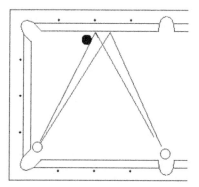

The use of English can change this angle also. Side English has the most drastic capability of changing the angle. See Below, this ball was hit with right English applied to the ball so once it hit the rail it spun off to the right.

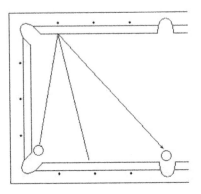

As you can see it drastically changed our natural angle!

So what can change an angle? Yep you guessed it. Everything! Which is why banking is one of the most difficult shots in the game of pool. Stroke, speed, top English, bottom English, left English, right English, the rotation of the earth must be just right to make a bank. Not that they can't be made, oh no, once a person has mastered how to hit the cue ball and the object ball, banks become much easier to perform.

Most people hit banks hard, to try to make them although this works just as well as anything else. You must realize that by hitting it hard you are not following the natural angle so you must over bank it to make it. Trying the natural angle requires the ball be hit smoothly and accurately.

Tips on improving your game

The Power Break:

The break is a whole different shot than any other on the table. If you don't get a good break, the chances of making a ball on the break plummet. The more the balls scatter the higher the chance of a ball going into a pocket. So lets discuss how to get a powerful break.

Place the cue ball just under the first diamond, rest your cue stick on the table, put your front hand over it with the cue between your first finger and your middle finger. Curl your fingers under the rail, now rock back and forth just a little while stroking, when ready to shoot rock forward and step forward with the front foot while stroking through the hit. This will add some body weight to it and give you a very powerful break.

After the Break:
Even the most seasoned player occasionally makes this mistake, choosing the wrong set of balls to start with. Choosing the wrong set can doom your game to failure from the beginning. Where choosing the right set can lead to table run after table run.

When approaching an open table you must look for the hard shots, the trapped balls, the open balls the breakout shots, all these must be considered before choosing to take the solids or stripes in the game of 8-Ball.

In the next couple of diagrams we will look at a few scenarios. And discuss which is the best set to shoot for. In the following diagrams, the gray balls will represent stripes and the black balls will represent the solids.

Example 1:

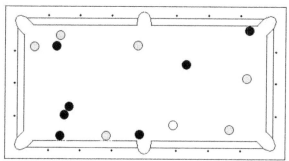

In the scenario above, it seems real obvious, we take the stripes (gray balls), one ball was already made for us, and we have a perfect shot shooting one in the corner, and it sets up for our next shot just great.

All is not quite as easy as it looks. Sure you can run all the stripes out fairly easily, except for that one on the rail. It has no pocket to go into.. Any attempt at breaking it out will, most likely wind up breaking out the solids for your opponent. Sure you can try to bank it in the side, but if you miss... its game over! Because banking it will likely wind up breaking the solids out again.

Ok but the solids have two balls stuck together and are spread all over the table, so why the solids? Two things, the first being they are spread out, so you have several shots to choose from. The second, is that those balls that are tied together have two natural break-out shots available. Lets look closer.

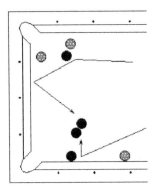

So with these two break-out shots available the chances of running the solids are much higher.

Scenario #2

Lets look at another scenario, it's a really bad break, it's open table and most the balls are clumped together in the center of the table, no-ones going to run this table, so now what?

Example 2:

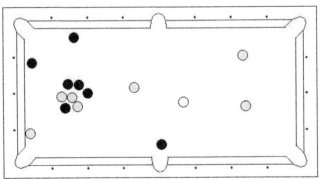

Oh come on, this is so obvious! The stripes (gray balls) have 4 open balls while the solids have 4 clustered balls. So we have to take the stripes.

Again all is not as it seems, with some simple strategy we can change the outlook of this game drastically! First we shoot the solid ball in the side pocket to guarantee the balls we want, rolling the cue ball forward to get the next shot.

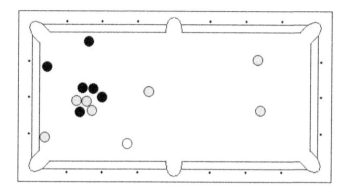

Now we play our strategy, hitting the top ball in the cluster scatters our balls while leaving his! Hit the front ball with a little low English on the cue to stick it right there and now look at the game

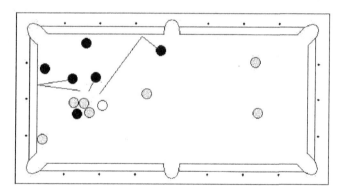

Now the table is in our favor, we leave the opponent without a shot, he now has three balls trapped by our ball, and our balls are out in the open ready to be picked off one by one. When we get closer to the last ball we go for our break-out and run the rest of the table.

Planning for the simple run:

Methodical planning of your shot strategy can only go so far. You must be flexible when an unexpected roll of the cue ball happens. When looking at a table, examine all the pockets available for each ball, the balls that have only one pocket they can go into will be your trouble balls. Any ball trapped by your opponents' balls will be a trouble ball.

These factors make up your shot strategy for the game. You need to design your strategy around breaking out those trapped balls as well as getting that one pocket shot for your trouble balls.

This uses the things you have learned with your English and some skill to run a table completely from break to last ball. Let's look in depth on a table at each ball and our choices we have, then we will come up with a shot strategy that will work the best for us.

Our Scenario:

Our opponent almost ran the table on us. He left us with six balls scattered on the table, how do we run this table with out breaking up his balls he has trapped? We want to keep it easy, and use the least amount of English as possible.

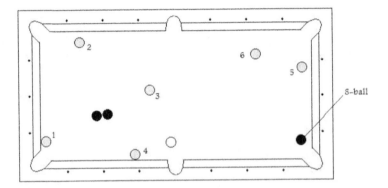

First we look at where each ball can be pocketed. We avoid thinking of banks or trying to squeeze into position behind a ball to shoot it all the way to the other side of the table. Instead think of the easiest places for the balls to go.

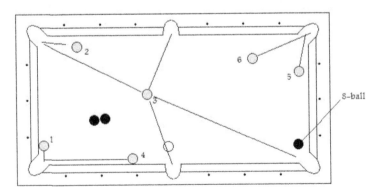

The #1 ball only has the one pocket it can be easily made into. The #2 ball has only on pocket also. The #3 ball has several pockets it can go into. The #4 ball must go down the rail to the corner, (on most tables, shooting a ball down the rail past the side pocket will not work). #5 ball and the #6 ball have the same one pocket to go to.

Now which one is our hardest ball to make, that would be ball #4, it is on a rail three diamonds away from the pocket. So #4 is our critical shot we must have good positioning on it to make it. Well our cue ball is in pretty good position now and we have the #1 ball as a funnel to help our ball in if we miss it really badly, so what if we shoot it now?

Ok lets look at that what will happen if we shoot it now. Now remember we are going to be shooting with no English and just hard enough to make it, unless otherwise specified.

We shoot the 4 down the rail, just hard enough to make it.

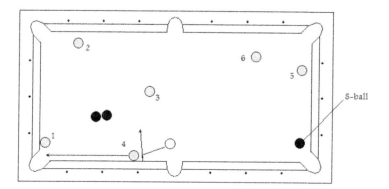

This works out good. If we missed the 4, he has nothing to shoot at, but we made it. Now we can shoot the 3 in the side.

If we had rolled to far for this shot, we could have shot the #2 ball, or if it rolled way to far we simply shoot the #3 ball in the other side pocket. But since we did what we planned on doing we shoot the #3 in the side nice and easy.

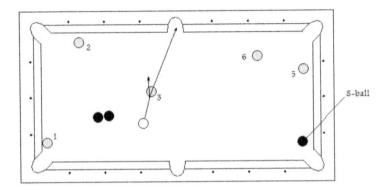

The cue ball wound up in a place that's good for two different balls, the #6 and the #2 ball. And if we missed our opponent still has nothing to shoot at. But the best shot is the #2 ball it is an easy shot and leaves us for our #1 ball.

We shoot the #2 ball with just enough power to make it this will allow the cue ball to bounce of the rail enough for us to shoot. This is the only point where we leave some kind of shot for our opponent, but it was an easy shot for our #2 ball so we did not miss

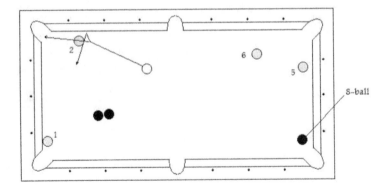

Now we have a good easy shot for our #1 ball we will shoot this one with a little bit of force, (not a lot of force, your not slamming it).

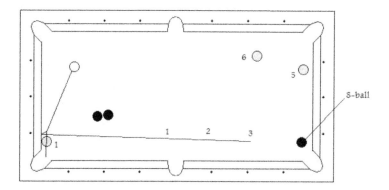

Now if we stopped in the #1 position we shoot the 6 ball first, if you shot it too hard and wound up the #2 position we still shoot the #6 ball, only if we got way to far like the #3 position do we then change our shot to shoot in the #5 ball. In any of these cases we leave no shot for our opponent.

In the illustration below the black line is the path of the cue ball when shooting from the #1 position at the #6 ball. To shoot this shot we need to use the same amount of force we shot the #1 ball with, again we are not slamming it, just hitting it firmly.

The red line represents the cue ball path when shot from the #2 position for the #6 ball, in this position we shoot with a little less force than what we used one the #1 ball. The blue line represents the #3 position shooting at the #5 ball we need to shoot this with a little less force than what we used on the #1 ball. Again we left no shot for our opponent.

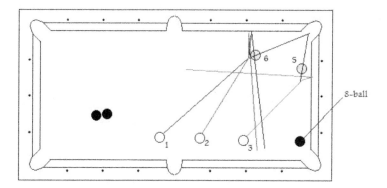

As you can see the #1 and #2 positions leave virtually the same shot for the #5 ball, and nothing for our opponent.

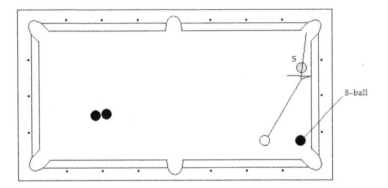

Now after our shot on the #5 ball the 8-ball is and easy shot, now we just ran a table without using any English and very little skill. We used natural rolls to take us right to where we needed to be, making it look very easy, (like a pro). We used another strategy that was not discussed yet but I might as well reveal it now. "Shooting in a Circle", let me show you what I mean. We shot the balls in order 4, 3, 2 then 1.

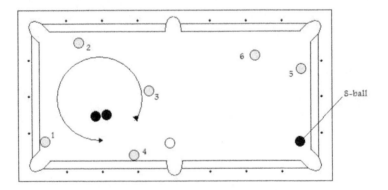

Shooting in a circle instead of zigzagging all over the table will allow you to shoot with natural rolls and not have to require English to help get your positioning. Shooting in a circle pattern usually allows for lighter shots to be done and not slamming balls around! Plus you get a little exercise walking around the table.

Using the Bridge Stick:

Do not be afraid of using a bridge, it's not un-manly to use the "Granny Stick". It's part of the game just as safeties are, so get used to it. A good pool player is just as comfortable using the bridge as they are using there own hand as a bridge. The bridge and proper holding techniques will make sure you make that shot. How many times have you seen someone stretched out over the table trying to hit a ball only to miscue?! Well here is how to use the bridge.

The following photos show the proper way to hold the bridge and your cue for a shot.

Your arm should be straight up and down as much as possible, this gives you better alignment and more feeling for the strength used in the shot. Stroke the shot using forward strokes of not more than 6-8 inches with at least another 4 inches of follow through on the hit.

FOR ADVANCED SHOOTERS

The 8-Ball Break:

Most everyone knows you shoot from the side and hitting the second ball (the so called 8-ball break) has a very good chance at making the 8-ball on the break. But most people don't know how to increase that chance of making it tenfold. In the diagram below we see how to decide which side to break it from to increase your chance. Look at the rack, line up the two end rail center diamonds and examine the positioning of the rack.

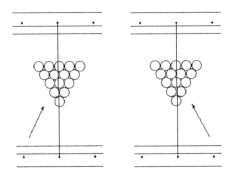

In these diagrams the balls are racked straight but not centered. So you break from the side you have the best chance of hitting the second ball more fully.

In the diagrams below we see the balls were racked slightly askew. The first ball is on the dot, but we see the line does not go thru the center of the rack. Again by lining up the diamonds we chose the side that has the better view of the second ball.

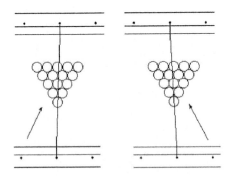

When we break we must hit the ball with low English, hitting the second ball as close to the first ball as possible without touching it. If you even barely skim the head ball you'll scratch.

Ok but what if it is racked perfectly centered? Well, then it's really a choice of which side you prefer breaking from, however your aiming changes slightly. In the diagram on the next page we see the point to aim at.

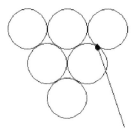

Now what you are aiming at is the point where the second and third ball contact each other. As you can see this is a very risky location and will lead to a lot of scratches if enough bottom English is not applied. No matter what side you shoot from the cue goes in the same location, just behind the head string about 1/2 a ball off the rail.

Hard Shot vs. Easy Shot:
We've all done it, we look at a table and pass up an easy shot cause if we can just make the hard one we can run the rest of the table. But think about it why is this shot a "hard" one, in most cases it's because we are not in the right position.

So remember this, never pass up an easy shot for a hard one, take the easy one and use your English to get a better position on the "hard" one. I have watched countless people make this same mistake over and over again.

Breakouts:
When going for a breakout, don't wimp out!! Use enough force to breakout your ball(s) AND your cue ball. This is a mistake made over and over again, sure they get the breakout but then wind up with no shot because they did not get the cue ball back out also. So use enough force to scatter the balls and roll out.

Safeties:
Safeties are part of the game, get used to it! A good safety will win the game when all seems lost. Remember your opponent can't win if he doesn't have that 8-ball shot. Even in games that do not have "safeties" as a rule does not mean you can't use them, a "Safety" simply means I'm giving up my shot and trying not to give you one.

One other thing about shooting a safety. If your going to shoot a safety try helping yourself out, don't shoot a safety just to shoot a safety. For example, you have two balls tied together and your going to hide the cue ball behind them then at least break them up enough to be able to make them both when you get the next shot don't make things worse by just simply hiding behind them.

Hiding behind two balls that are tied up:

Having two balls tied up together may not be such a bad thing. Some times they can be used to hide the cueball. In the example below, we have two balls tied together none of your balls can be pocketed. Your opponent has just missed the eight ball, it's hanging in the pocket your two balls are tied together, this seems like all is lost.

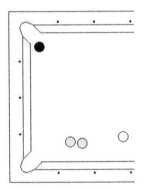

Don't panic, there is an excellent safety here. Hitting the cueball softly at the side of the first ball the cue ball rolls to the rail and is hidden behind the first ball. (Use the Natural roll angle you learned before to know where to hit the object ball)

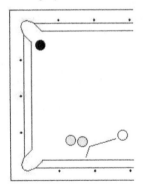 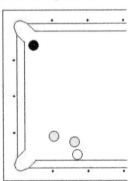

The energy from the cue ball is transferred to the first ball then to the second ball. The first ball stops dead and the second one rolls a little, now they spread apart for you to easily make them on your next shot. You now turned a sure loss into a win for you!

Hiding behind two balls out on the open table:

It is possible to hide your cueball behind another ball out in the middle of the table. In the example below the same type of scenario is going on. The opponent has only the eight ball left you have two balls that can not be made and tied up together.

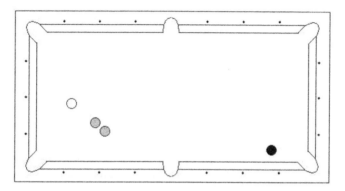

Using top English and a soft touch, we are going to hit the first ball as straight as possible into the second ball. The first ball will stop dead, the second ball will travel into the rail, now the cue ball with the top English will want to continue forward right into the first ball hiding right behind it. The results of the shot are shown here:

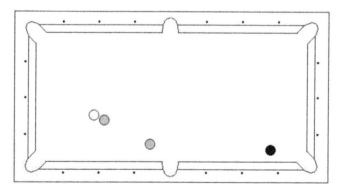

These examples have been with two balls lined up roughly with the cue ball. Well what if they aren't lined up? It's a simple answer, but it's also a little harder shot to perform.

Hiding the cue behind another ball:
In the example below the cueball has been moved to represent this

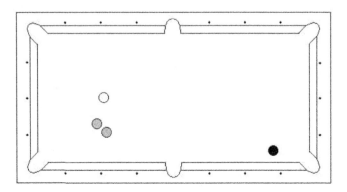

In this shot we shoot at the object ball so that the cue ball rolls forward and hides behind the second ball. Shooting directly at the object ball (in this case) with a small amount of forward english moves the object ball to the rail and the cue ball rolls behind the second ball. Below is the result of this shot;

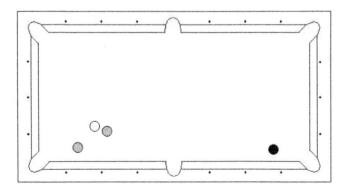

In each of these examples you have now successfully hidden the eightball from your opponent. He will have to try a wild shot to even hit it. If he scratches while attempting to hit it you win. If he misses the eightball shot now you have your balls broken out away from each other and can now run the rest of them out and win that way. Safeties are part of a winning strategy! Use them when needed, remember the more balls he runs out the more places you can hide the cueball from him.

Masse' Shots:
   Masse' shots, or curve shots do not mean jack your stick over your head and slam the ball. A masse' shot can be done with as little a lifting of the back end of the stick up another 5 inches above normal.
   In General, the longer the shot curve is, the lower the stick can be. A masse' is done when the side of the cue ball is hit, this tilting of the axis of spin causes a curving motion to the cue ball. Longer shots with very little curve needed can be done as simply as putting low, left or right English with a slightly lifted rear end of the stick.

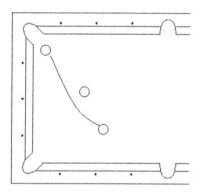

   The drawing above shows a typical masse' shot.

   One drawback to the masse shot is that they are hard to control and another is that once the curve is complete it is now top English, and in most cases follows the object ball for several inches after the hit.

   Aiming location when looking down at the ball for a right hand Masse' Shot

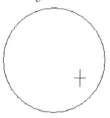

Hitting a Masse' shot;
   Starting out at 75 degrees from the table, this angle of shot should provide a curve radius of just a few inches, roughly a two balls length. Use this when a tight curve is

needed to move around a blocking ball. Usually when the ball is blocking around 3/4 of your object ball.

The hit is done as if your are shooting low left or low right English, depending on the curve needed, but with the stick at the 75 degree angle and looking down on the ball. Be very careful not to slam your cue tip into the table trying this shot.

The next illustration shows a tight curve being done around the ball to sink the object ball

A Tight Masse' Shot:

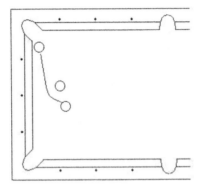

Dropping down to 50-60 degrees gives a curve of about 3 balls or ~6 inches. This is for most curves when shooting across a table, and the blocking ball is blocking your shot by about 1/2 the ball.

General Purpose Masse' Shot:

Dropping to 40 degrees is the prime zone; this angle depending on the power can give a radius of 6 inches to 3 feet. This is generally used when a blocking ball is not too close to the cue and the object ball is between 2 feet to 4 feet away. When hit firmly the curve will occur within the first 12" and straighten out. When hit hard the curve will be elongated to around 16" then straighten out

Long Range Masse' Shot

Dropping down to about 25 degrees is for the long masse' shots they will spin out within the first 1 foot or so then straighten out, this is used the ball is only blocked by a small amount, ~ 1/4 of the ball. These are used when the ball is far away and you need only a small curve to get around the blocking ball. The cue stick being around 25 degrees is low enough to allow a more precise aiming.

Aiming a Masse' shot:

The only aiming you can do on a masse shot is to aim enough to the side of the blocking ball to clear it once you hit the cue ball. The Masse' shot will start out straight on the direction you shot it, then the curve will start to take and alter its direction.

A Long Range Masse' shot

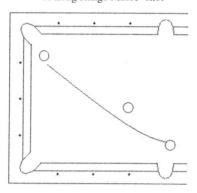

Jump Shots:

A jump shot is not scooping the ball by hitting the table first right at the bottom of the ball. A legal jump shot is actually a forcing of the cue ball to bounce off the table by hitting the ball very firmly above the centerline with a loose grip on the cue stick.

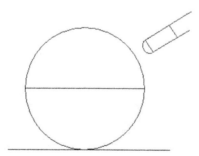

The previous drawing shows the centerline of the cue ball and a cue stick hitting at approximately 40 degrees.

55

This can be done with a regular pool cue or a "Jump Stick". In either case to get the cue ball to jump, enough force must be applied to the top half of the ball and the stick bounce out of the way before the cue rises from the table. This requires some finesse.

The grip on the stick must be loose; this allows the stick to bounce back out of the way. The force to the cue ball must be very firm and in a snapping motion. If your grip is too tight on the stick, the cue ball will simply "squirt" out from under your stick.

The angle used is in proportion to how short or long you need it to hop. The higher the angle the stick is held at the shorter the hop. Usually the stick is somewhere within the 70 to 40 degree range.

A cue stick can jump a cue ball over the "edge" of a ball by simply raising your stick to around 20 to 25 degrees and hitting the cue ball firmly, just above the centerline as shown below.

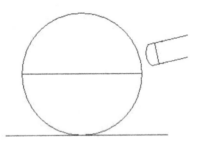

Throwing a Ball:

Ever had 2 balls touching each other that look like they are lined up perfectly to go into the pocket, but then you hit the first ball and the second ball misses the pocket. Well chances are they were lined up just fine but the way you hit the first ball "threw" the second one out of the pocket.

Throwing a ball is using the friction between the two touching balls to change the path of the second ball. During the time the two balls are in contact with each other they can be pushed into an alternate path. As the first ball passes thru it is pushing the second ball forward and to the side, until they finally separate.

The most amount of throw can be applied when it is the cue ball that is touching the object ball to be thrown. In the next drawing we see how two balls lined up along one path can be thrown to the side.

When ball #1 is shot to the right, ball #2 is thrown to the right, when shot from the left it will be thrown to the left. This effect will also happen when the cue hits ball #1. If the cue ball hits ball #1 on the left side, ball #2 will be thrown to the right. Likewise, if the cue ball hits the right side of ball #1, ball #2 goes to the left.

When the cue ball is the one frozen to the object ball shooting left and right English can magnify the throw to almost two diamonds down the length of a table. The average "throw" is about 1 diamond down the length of a table, about 1/2 diamond shooting side to side on a table.

Making that pesky Ball off the Rail Shot:

Remembering that a rail is to be used just like a mirror it should be possible to make a ball by shooting the cue ball off the rail, and do it pretty reliably.

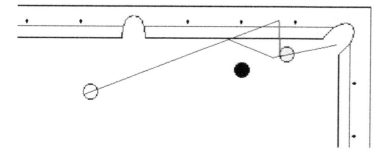

Using our stick we measure the distance from the point of contact to the rail, then that exact same distance from the rail out, we look to the cue ball from this point to find our spot to aim at. The cue will bounce off the rail and make the ball a vast majority of the time.

If we can't get to the spot we need to hit we can use English to change that angle we come off the rail. If you have to aim past your spot on the rail, use bottom English to come off the rail at a sharper angle. If you must aim before your spot, use top English to flatten out the angle. Each one of these types of English will change your angle slightly. Also if your leave for the next shot requires some kind of English be used, you can aim before or after the spot to adjust the shot for the English being used.

Double Rail Shots:

Using two rails to hit your ball is a skill you will need. Sometimes a using single rail will not get you to your object ball. You'll need to know how to plan a two rail shot. Below is a diagram showing a shot. The white cue ball has been hidden from the gray ball, you must hit your ball or a foul will be called.

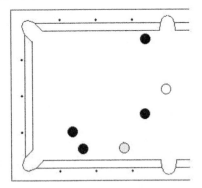

To align the shot first use your cue stick to get the centerline. Set your cue stick centered between the cue ball and the object ball, point it directly at the center of the pocket where the two rails would meet. See below:

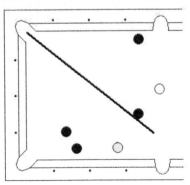

You now must shoot parallel to the cue stick, the arrows show the path of the cue ball.

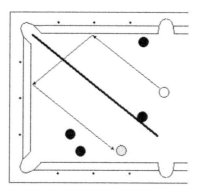

This shot requires precise measurement and practice to do with any kind of reliability.

Caroms:

Caroms look like hard shots but in reality they aren't that hard when you know the secrets. So what are the secrets to carom shots? Well if you read this book from start to now you already know them, you just didn't know you knew them.

A carom is nothing more than using principles I have already explained, in a way a little different than how I showed them to you before. The principles we are going to use are the ones we saw when we were doing the cue ball positioning.

The "90 degrees" this is about 50 percent of the caroms out there. Let's take a look. In the next diagram we see a typical 90 degree carom. The black ball is blocking our shot to the pocket, but we have another ball close so we can carom off of it.

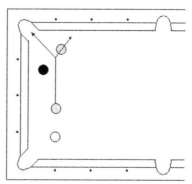

This is a relatively easy shot to do and easy to line up. Using your cue stick we want to figure out where the object ball needs to carom off our other ball. Simply take your cue stick and lay it next to the ball pointing into the high side of the pocket, like in the next drawing.

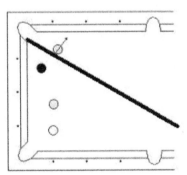

Take the cue stick and move it closer to the ball we are caroming off of, the point where the cue stick would touch the ball is the exact point we shoot at for our point of contact. If we shoot the ball lightly into the other ball and they make contact on this point it will carom off directly into the pocket.

Now you said the "90 degree" rule is about 50% of the carom shots out there, why? Well, remember how we changed directions of the cue ball off the object ball using English, We can even use english on an object ball!! So now is a good time to talk about "Transference".

Transference:
When you hit the cue ball with bottom English and it is still spinning when it hits the object ball some of that spin is transferred to the object ball. So in other words if you hit the cue with backspin, the object ball will get some topspin transferred to it. Likewise if topspin is on the cue ball the object ball will get backspin.

Using this "Transference" we can change this "90 degree" angle to what we need.

Transference Diagram:

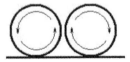

In the above drawing we see that the cue ball on the left was hit with low English, causing it to spin counter clockwise. Once the object ball on the right is hit some friction from the spinning ball causes the object ball to get some of that transferred spin. This causes a top spin on the object ball.

Given the carom shot in the next diagram, we see the object ball is in the section where it is almost a straight shot at the second ball so using the knowledge we learned before, the caroming ball should approximately follow the thick line, and there by missing the shot.

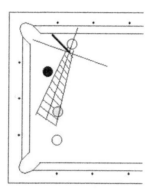

Ok, here is where we can make the transference work for us. Shoot the ball exactly the same as if it was a regular "90 degree" carom shot as far as the point of contact is concerned. But the difference is your going to shoot top English on the cue ball transferring bottom to the object ball. This will make the object ball carom off the second ball at a different angle more in back of the thicker line and towards the pocket, making the carom shot.

This kind of shot is usually shot very firmly so that enough of the English gets transferred to the object ball, and so that the English lasts long enough to reach the ball we are caroming off of. Since it is shot so firmly and is relying on a lot of factors to work it is a low percentage shot. Consider shooting a safety as we talked about earlier.

Transference can also come from a rail, when a ball comes off a rail at a shallow angle some sidespin is picked up from the rail as shown below.

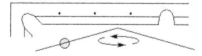

Since the ball hit the rail and bounced off it picked up a small amount of sidespin.

This transference is also a great tool for another kind of carom shot that comes up quite a bit. It's a shot where you play the object ball off of a rail into another ball to carom your shot in to the corner pocket.

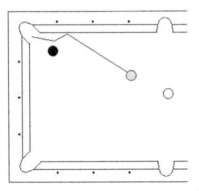

In this diagram, the shot to the corner is blocked by an opponent's ball. But by using the techniques we learned we can easily make this shot.

First we use the 90 degree technique to find the point of contact off our opponents ball into the pocket, then the mirror technique to find where we aim our object ball on the rail to hit off the rail into the opponent's ball. Now we shoot the shot with bottom on the cue ball.

So how does this work? Bottom on the cue puts top on the object ball, the rail puts a slight amount of side English to it, once the object ball hits the opponents ball the side and forward forces the object ball to continue rolling forward, right into the pocket!

Action and Reaction:

Getting that next shot depends on the English you used in the first shot. In this section we are going to talk about the cue ball reactions after hitting the object ball. In the proceeding chapters we talked about the basics of English. Forward makes it go forward, backspin make it come back, but what about shooting reverse English and side English, or top and side. For example when shooting low left English the ball spins in an axis displayed in the drawing below as it travels forward.

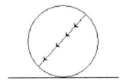

What are the physics behind the cueball's reactions. In all shots where there is an angle to be shot the cue ball, once it contacts the object ball, will change it's axis a small amount. This axis changes when it hits the object ball, or a rail. For example straight reverse English becomes top English if the cue ball is shot directly into a rail. Any other angle to the rail causes the axis to shift somewhat and alter the cue balls reactions. For purposes of teaching we are going to assume an angle of 45 degrees or more for the following example.

The following diagram shows a typical shot into the side pocket, in this shot we want to break out our ball for a possible next shot.

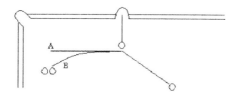

Using No English at all, the path of the ball is approximately Path "A". Shooting Low English will not get it to follow path "B" as you would hope. Instead it will follow path "A" again. This is due to the cue balls reaction after hitting the object ball. The only way for the cue ball to follow path "B" is if the shot is less than 45 degrees, but again we are talking about thin cuts of greater than 45 degrees. So how can we break out those balls? Well here is where knowing the cue balls reaction helps. Putting low right or left will put almost solid left or right on the ball. This breakout is done with low left English.

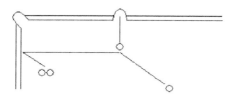

The Cue balls reaction after hitting the object ball is that the low will be cancelled out leaving only left on the cue ball. So when the cue ball touches the rail the left then spins into the balls breaking them out.

For All Players

Cue Stick Maintenance:

A Cue stick can be a rather expensive investment, ranging from $40 to $1600. So care should be given to the cue stick. Your cue stick should be kept inside a case and in a cool dry place. Moisture and heat can warp a cue stick until it is unusable. A hard case is a better choice than a soft case as the hard cases tend to allow less warping.

The cue tip however, is a disposable item. It does wear out and periodically needs replacement. Since the tip is made from leather it can be smashed down until it is as hard as a rock. Frequent chalking as discussed earlier in the book will make the tip last longer and keep you from miscuing.

"Scuffing" the Tip:

"Scuffing up" of the tip should be done before prolonged use. Many scuffing materials are sold most are simply a gritty material or a group of spikes. They are designed to disturb the tip causing the smashed material to fluff up. This allows the chalk to coat the material better allowing for better contact with the cue ball. The process of fluffing up the tip will cause layers of the tip to be lost until the tip becomes thin.

When the tip gets too thin the material will not absorb the shock of hitting the cue ball and will result in the ferrule breaking. The ferrule is the material on the end of the stick that the tip is attached to. When your tip gets too thin (~ 3/16 thick) replace it.

The Shape of the Tip:

The shape of the tip should be like the edge of a nickel. Too round and you will not be able to shoot accurately, too flat and you will not be able to get English.

Removing Dings in the Shaft:

Everyone gets them, those little dings in the shaft of your cue stick. They come from dropping your cue, to accidentally hitting your cue stick against something. To remove them take a washcloth, dip it into boiling hot water and wrap it around the shaft where the ding is. The heat and the moisture will swell the wood back out filling in the ding.

Practice Games

To practice our skills this is a game I came up with. It works on your ability to cut balls down the rail, and your English skills. The object of the game is to make each ball on the first shot, and the cue ball cannot touch any ball other than the one you are currently shooting. You get 15 shots to make all the balls. The game is concluded when all fifteen shots have been taken or the cue ball has touched another ball.

For beginners, try only to not touch any other ball with your cue ball, other than the one your shooting you can miss shots but you must control your cue ball! Once the cue ball touches another ball count how many shots it took or how many balls are left, use this as a scorecard to measure if you're getting better.

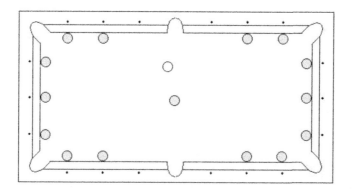

This is old classic, in this game your allowed to put the cue ball anywhere you want to, you get 15 shots to make every ball on the table.

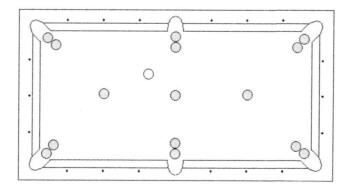

Some hints about shooting this game:

Hint #1: If you'll notice the balls are right in front of the pockets starting out. So a nice easy hit will make one ball and leave the other right in front of the pockets

Hint #2: If you hit the balls in front of the side pocket, from where the cue ball is in the drawing below, gently right on the top of the second ball the cue ball will roll down the rail and knock a ball into the corner also! Giving you one extra shot!

Thank you for reading my book I hope what I had to offer you improved your game. I wish you many happy games of pool.

Printed in Great Britain
by Amazon